CONTENTS

GROSS SMELLS

Shrek's swamp is muddy and smelly – and that's the way he likes it! These whiffy wonders would be right up his street ...

When it comes to pleasant smells, flowers are up there with perfume, right? Wrong! Not all blooms smell good! One flower in particular is super-pongy!

The corpse flower (Rafflesia arnoldii) is a rare plant found in the rainforests of Indonesia and gives off a *seriously* revolting smell, like piles of rotting meat!

This weird whiffer can grow really big – sometimes up to a metre across – and can weigh more than a bowling ball.

Believe it or not, the corpse flower's pong actually attracts insects, which pollinate the plant. Just goes to show there's no accounting for taste when it comes to smelly stuff!

DID YOU KNOW?

When you breathe in, tiny molecules of chemicals (odours) enter your nostrils and pass through slimy mucus inside your nose. Tiny hairs, called cilia, recognize the different smells!

Pongy corpse flower

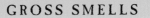

STINK SPEAK

Wherever you go in the world, now you'll be able to say
"that stinks!" in 15 different languages ...

"Dat stinkt!"
Dutch

"Esse fedores!"
Portugese

"At stinker!"
Danish

"Ce puanteurs!"
French

"Det stinker!"
Swedish

"Ze smrdi!"
Czech

"Dieses gestank!"
German

"Yang menyebalkan!"
Indonesian

"Bod stinks!"
Welsh

"Ese apesta!"
Spanish

"Ez a büdös!"
Hungarian

"Kwamba stinks!"
Swahili

"Che puzza!"
Italian

"Na stinks!"
Filipino

"Bu kokuyor!"
Turkish

STINKERAMA!

Most people like the smell of fresh fruit but one fruity whiff you *won't* like is the durian fruit. It smells like stale vomit mixed with mouldy cheese. The stink is so gross that in some parts of the world, it's illegal to cut it open in public!

Stinky durian fruit

Your nose can tell the difference between 10,000 smells!

The Madeira cockroach makes a super-stink to frighten away predators. The stench it conjures up has been compared to a whole butcher's shop of rotting meat.

The smelliest frog is the Venezuela skunk frog. This hoppy little stinker warns off its enemies by releasing a whiffy chemical, identical to the one produced by skunks!

Body odour (BO) does not come from sweat. People get BO when bacteria on our skin mixes with the sweat we produce, and releases stinky chemicals.

TRUE OR FALSE?
The posh word for your sense of smell is pongfulsion.
Answer: False!
Your sense of smell is also called olfaction.

They may look cute, but skunks are one of the smelliest mammals in the world. The fluffy little furballs are famous for the stinking yellow liquid they spray to deter predators!

A skunk's stink is produced by glands under its tail. The skunk flips round when threatened and blasts its foe with a foul-smelling mist that can linger for days and be smelled from half-a-mile.

If you meet a skunk, stand back – they can spray their whiffy scent as far as 3 metres!

Even skunks seem to know their musk smells horrible – they won't spray in confined spaces or their own den unless they really have to.

DID YOU KNOW?
Once the odour has been removed, the skunk's musk is used in perfume to make it last longer.

Smelly skunk →

9

The South American hoatzin may just be the world's whiffiest bird. It's known as the 'stink turkey' because it pongs of cow manure!

TRUE OR FALSE?
Some perfumes smell of cow manure!

Answer: True! The smell is known to perfumers (the people who make perfume) as animallic. Cows would moo if they knew!

The four smelliest areas of the human body are:

1. underarms
2. feet
3. mouth
4. scalp

The zorilla is a skunk-like creature that lives in Africa. When this little guy gets scared, it sprays a stinking liquid out from under its tail to scare off predators! The stench can be detected up to 1 kilometre away!

Our smell is as individual as our fingerprint or DNA.

Some people don't have a sense of smell – this is known as anosmia.

It doesn't matter how smelly your feet are, mosquitoes will be attracted to the enzymes on them.

Whiffy hoatzins

Lots of us like mushroom soup, but no one would want to eat soup made from stinkhorn mushrooms. Covered with a thick, greenish-black, shiny layer of spore slime, these mushrooms don't just look revolting, they stink of dead meat and dirty toilets!

Epoisses de Bourgogne cheese is so smelly, it's illegal to take it on public transport in France.

Eating lots of certain foods, like garlic, onions and curry, means that your BO will last longer. This is because they contain chemicals that stay longer in sweat.

The burrowing owl makes its nest underground and lines it with smelly cow dung – must smell *lovely* in there!

Farts smell thanks to the chemicals indole and skatole, which pop up when germs work on protein from your food.

DID YOU KNOW?
One 1.5kg pat of pongy elephant dung can contain up to 16,000 dung beetles. And these little bugs have a *really* strong sense of smell!

TOP 15 GROSS SHREK SMELLS

There are tons of stinky smells in the Shrek movies, but which ones are the smelliest? Check out the 15 whiffiest wafts here ...

15 MUDDY MESS
Shrek loves relaxing in mud pools. And they smell as good as they look!

14 FERMENTING FEET
Overgrown toenails and bad bathing habits mean Shrek's feet smell foul!

13 BREATHE IT IN
A diet of raw onions, swamp slugs and swamp toad soup mean Shrek's breath stinks – gargling with swamp mud probably doesn't help!

12 STINKIN' SIPPER
Forget fruit juice or water, Shrek's tipple is an eyeballtini. They look gross and smell rancid too!

11 SWEATY SWAMP
Surrounded by gloopy mud pools and fungus-filled trees, Shrek's swamp is probably the stinkiest place in the enchanted forest. That's why he loves it so much!

10 FOUL FOOD
Shrek and Fiona love nothing better than tucking into weedrat stew – something that has to be smelled to be believed!

9 WHIFFY WIND
Ogre babies burp and fart even more than regular babies, and Shrek and Fiona both love letting rip too. There's always lots of stinky gas in Shrek's house!

8 RANCID ROAR
When Shrek roars, look out for the spray of smelly food and stinky spit!

7 VOM-DERFUL!

Most babies are often sick after they've eaten (yuck!). Unfortunately for Shrek and Fiona, ogre baby vomit smells really bad!

6 CHEESY DOES IT!

It's no wonder that Gorder, one of the Three Blind Mice, thought he'd found some cheese when he climbed on Shrek's shoulder. Shrek's lughole smells horribly cheesy!

5 TOILET TROUBLES

Blocked toilets never smell very nice, but when an ogre's outhouse get clogged up, the stench is eye-wateringly bad.

4 NOXIOUS NAPPIES

Ogre babies produce a lot of poop! The pail outside Shrek and Fiona's house is full of dirty nappies so steer clear if you can!

3 HUMMING HOUSE

With swamp rats hanging on the wall and jars of eyeballs everywhere, it's no wonder Shrek's house is horribly smelly. Luckily, he and his family love it that way!

2 STAR STINKER

He may shower every now and then, but being an ogre means Shrek is guaranteed to pong! After all, he does shower in stinky mud ...

1 SMELLY SITE

If Shrek and his family smell bad, imagine how a whole army of ogres would whiff? That's right, the ogre army campsite is one big pongfest!

Next time you tuck into a cheese sandwich, just hope it's not Stinking Bishop. This cheese won Britain's Smelliest Cheese Championships and seriously whiffs!

The wolverine might look cute but this critter oozes foul fluid to mark its territory. The disgusting musk has earned it the nicknames 'skunk bear' and 'nasty cat'.

Wolverine

TRUE OR FALSE?

Your sense of smell gets worse as you get older?

Answer: True! Kids have a much stronger sense of smell than their parents or grandparents.

Feet have more sweat glands than any other part of the body, which means they can get super-sweaty! Unfortunately, if we're wearing shoes, the sweat can't evaporate, so it hangs about getting smelly until we wash our feet.

Bull elephants are extremely dangerous when their body produces too much male hormone. They end up in a state called 'musth', with a gross smell oozing from glands on their foreheads, and will attack anything! Luckily they smell so bad, no one wants to be very close to them!

Ever noticed a nasty niff coming from someone's mouth as they speak? Nearly everyone has bad breath (halitosis) at some stage, and it's all caused by smelly bacteria …

14

Keeping your teeth clean helps keep your breath fresh because it gets rid of bacteria, called plaque, which builds up in your mouth.

Decaying food trapped between your teeth can also cause bad breath. If you don't brush, the tiny bits of food caught in your teeth start to rot which doesn't smell nice at all!

Brushing your teeth after you've eaten something smelly doesn't stop you getting bad breath. This is because the smell is coming from your lungs, not your mouth. The smelly bit of the food gets into your blood and when it reaches your lungs, it makes the air you breathe out smell.

If you could look at your tongue through a microscope, you'd see it's like a shaggy carpet, with millions

DID YOU KNOW?
Eating and drinking certain things is more likely to give you pongy breath, including garlic, onions, sweets and orange juice. And, if you're Shrek, swamp rats!

of filaments that trap tiny bits of food and bacteria. Brushing your tongue will help keep it clean!

Chewing gum helps keep your breath fresh because it produces saliva (spit), which helps wash away food particles and bacteria in your mouth.

Chewing gum

SWAMPED!

Star Tours all booked-up? No problem, come sightseeing now and see all the stinkiest spots at Shrek's swamp...

PONG ALERT!
The grassy roof on Shrek's home is packed with slimy soil, which smells *really* bad, just as he likes it!

PONG ALERT!
There's a lot of fungus in Shrek's swamp – this moss smells musty and damp!

PONG ALERT!
The mud pools that surround Shrek's house are pretty pongy – you probably won't want to dive into any of them for a soak!

16

PONG ALERT!
With all the gross slugs and swamp rats that get cooked in Shrek's house, it's best not to go too near his chimney!

PONG ALERT!
Steer clear of Shrek's outhouse It doesn't smell nice in there at the best of times, but it *really* stinks when the toilet gets blocked!

PONG ALERT!
With no glass in the windows, it's easy to smell the gross grime inside Shrek's house!

PONG ALERT!
The murky water in the swamp is covered in rancid algae and is seriously stinky!

SMELLY JOKES

1. What do you get if you cross
   a skunk with a dinosaur?
   A stinkosaurus!

2. What did the judge say to
   the skunk?
   "Odour in the courtroom!"

3. Who works in a department store
   selling perfumes?
   Frank Incense!

4. What has lots of legs and
   smells nice?
   A scent-ipede!

5. Why do giraffes have such
   long necks?
   Because their feet smell!

6. What smells, runs about, and
   lies around with its tongue
   hanging out?
   A pair of old trainers!

7. What do you call a fairy that
   hasn't washed?
   Stinkerbell!

8. How many rotten eggs were
   in the omelette?
   A phew!

9. What's big and grey and whiffs?
   A smellyphant!

10. What do you get if you cross a
    rotten egg with a giant gorilla?
    King Pong!

11. What do you call someone who doesn't wash?
    I don't know but you can smell them coming!

12. What smells bad, has four wheels and flies?
    A rubbish truck!

13. Why is perfume obedient?
    Because it's scent wherever it goes!

14. What's the smelliest city in America?
    Phew York!

15. Did you hear about the skunk's book?
    It was a best smeller!

16. What game really stinks?
    Ping Pong!

17. Which super-hero is smelly?
    Pooperman!

18. How do skunks smell?
    Terrible!

19. Why did the car pong?
    It was full of gas!

20. How do you stop a fish from smelling?
    Plug his nose!

Your sense of smell is 10,000 times more sensitive than your sense of taste. Must be why some things smell so bad!

The stink bug (also known as the shield bug) produces a stinky

Stink bug

substance from its thorax, between the first and second pairs of legs. The smell, which is like damp laundry that's been left in the washing machine for weeks, is created to whiff away predators.

Active volcanoes create tons of gas that smells like rotten eggs. No wonder the volcano surrounding the castle Fiona was in stank!

The musk ox marks its territory by weeing everywhere. Unfortunately

TRUE OR FALSE?
People drink coffee that comes from pongy animal poo?
Answer: Kind of true!
The coffee, which is really expensive, is made from coffee beans that have been eaten and pooed out by a luak (a cat-sized mammal from Indonesia).

lots of the smelly wee gets splashed on the animal's belly, which makes it pong too.

Next time you get a whiff of a perfume, bear in mind that some scents contain whale vomit (ambergris)!

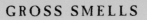

STINKY SMELLS QUIZ!

Now see how much you know about the world's worst whiffs . . .

1 How many different smells can your nose distinguish?
a) 1,000
b) 10,000
c) 100,000

2 Which fruit smells like stale sick and mouldy cheese?
a) Kiwi
b) Durian
c) Pong

3 What smelly stuff do burrowing owls line their nests with?
a) Cow dung
b) Rose petals
c) Used toilet roll

4 What does the corpse flower smell like?
a) Onions
b) Cabbages
c) Rotting meat

5 How far can skunks spray their whiffy musk?
a) 3 metres
b) 6 metres
c) 9 metres

6 Which insect makes a substance that smells like damp laundry?
a) Dragonfly
b) Bumblebee
c) Stink bug

7 The hairs in your nose that recognize smells are called?
a) Mucowts
b) Cilia
c) Ticklers

8 How many dung beetles can be found in elephant poo?
a) 16
b) 1,600
c) 16,000

Now turn over to see how you scored

ANSWERS

1b, 2b, 3a, 4c, 5a, 6c, 7b, 8c

UP TO 3 CORRECT

YOUR SCORE PONGS!

Not bad but you could learn more about the wide world of offensive odours. Give these pongin' pages another peek to brush up on your stinky knowledge.

4 TO 6 CORRECT

HEY, STINK STAR!

Well done! You may not know everything about the stomach-turning stinks Shrek and Fiona love, but you certainly know lots about the world's whiffiest odours!

OVER 7 CORRECT

YOU'RE A WHIFFY WONDER!

Wow! Is there no stench you can't sniff out? You must know all about the stinky stuff, just like Shrek. Take a deep breath and smell the sweet scent of success!

GROSS CREATURES

There are some pretty weird creatures in Shrek's swamp but
these creepy critters would give them a run for their money...

TOP 10
MOST COMMON CREEPY CRAWLIES*

1	Beetles	400,000
2	Ants, bees and wasps	250,000
3	Butterflies and moths	190,000
4	True flies	120,000
5	True bugs	100,000
6	Crickets, grasshoppers and locusts	20,000
7	Caddisflies	12,000
8	Lice	7,000
9	Dragonflies and damselflies	5,500
10	Lacewings	4,700

* By approximate number of known species

TRUE OR FALSE?
Nearly everyone eats insects.

Answer: Kind of true!
Many of us eat insects
without realizing it – the
red food colouring called
cochineal is made from the
dried bodies of a Mexican
cactus-eating insect.

Insects way outnumber human
beings. There are at least one
million of the creepy little critters
for each human on earth!

Insects called springtails live in the
topsoil all over the world. There
are probably as many as 600 million
per hectare (10,000 square metres).
Together they weigh more than the
entire human race.

In many countries insects are a
popular food. Insect dishes include
omelettes made from silkworms
and fried honeybees in
China, fried locusts in
Thailand and red ant
chutney in India. Mmmm,
don't they sound tasty?!

Maybe it's their gross
appearance or the way most of
them scuttle about? Maybe
it's the horrible crunching
sound they make when
you accidentally tread on
one? Whatever the reason,
it's a fact that creepy crawlies
gross most people out.

Cockroaches can live without food for up to a month. When they do eat a special set of teeth in their guts helps them digest food. Yum!

Science bods believe cockroaches are one of the oldest creatures on earth.

Cockroaches' brains are spread all over their body, which means they can live for at least a week without a head. They only die then because they can't drink anything!

There are over 5,000 species of cockroach.

A cockroach can hold its breath for up to 40 minutes. Gasp!

The world's largest cockroach lives in South America. It is 15cm long with a 30cm wingspan!

The German cockroach can survive for a whole year on just a single bar of soap!

Cockroaches have at least 18 knees. They also have tiny claws on their feet that mean they can scuttle up walls!

Creepy cockroaches

DID YOU KNOW?

Applying a crushed cockroach to a stinging wound will help relieve the pain.

25

Cow stomachs can hold 182 litres of food. That's enough to fill a whole bath – fancy a quick wash?!

The burps of 10 cows could keep a small house heated for a year. It wouldn't smell very nice in there though!

TRUE OR FALSE?
Some herbivores (plant-eaters) eat their own poo!
Answer: True! Herbivores find their diet hard to digest, so some of them have to eat their food twice!

When it comes to dinner, owls are speedy eaters. The feathery fiends mainly eat furry animals, such as mice and squirrels. If their prey is small enough, the owl will often swallow it whole and vomit up the bits they can't digest (like teeth, fur and claws) as pellets later.

Parrotfish sometimes make themselves a protective mucus sleeping bag, to keep predators and parasites away. Cosy!

The guanay cormorant is a bird that makes its nest extra cosy – by lining it with its own dried poo!

When sea cucumbers are attacked they have a super-gross way of dealing with it. The slug-like creatures squeeze their muscles and jettison some of their internal organs – out of their *bum*! Luckily, the missing body parts quickly grow back, but still ...

DID YOU KNOW?
Elephants' stomachs make so much noise when they're eating, they can stop their digestion at will if they think a predator might be near.

If a mouse gets hungry enough it will eat its own tail. Ouch!

Gross sea cucumber

The world's largest known frog, the goliath frog, lives in central Africa, measures up to 87.63cm long, and weighs as much as 3.66kg. What a w-*hopper*!

Some tortoises urinate on their back legs to stay cool. Best not try this at home ...!

Sharks protect their eyes by rolling them backwards when they attack prey. But how do they see where they're swimming?!

GROSS AWARDS!

Can't choose your favourite gross moment in a *Shrek* movie? Our special Gross Awards will help!

GROSS AWARD FOR MOST DISGUSTING SNACK

Forget candyfloss, Shrek loved it when Fiona collected flies with a spider's web for him to crunch on!
Film: *Shrek*
Gross rating: ●●●●●

GROSS AWARD FOR PUTTING OUT A FIRE

Shrek tries to put out the campfire when he and Donkey are on their quest to rescue Fiona, but stamping on it doesn't do the trick. So Donkey steps in and puts the fire out by *weeing* on it. Soggy!
Film: *Shrek*
Gross rating: ●●●

GROSS AWARD FOR MOST INVENTIVE BABY

When Fergus wants a new crayon, he just pulls a lump of yucky earwax from Shrek's ear and starts drawing with it. Bet that picture smells nice!
Film: *Shrek the Third*
Gross rating: ●●●●●

GROSS AWARD FOR MOST DISGUSTING GIFTS

Shrek sure knows how to charm people. When he's trying to get Fiona to fall in love with him again, he gives her a heart-shaped box of slugs and a skunk-scented candle!
Film: *Shrek Forever After*
Gross rating: ●●●●

GROSS CREATURES

GROSS AWARD FOR BAD TABLE MANNERS

Shrek accidentally swallowed his spoon when he was having dinner with Fiona's parents. When he coughed it up, the spoon flew across the dinner table, leaving a trail of green spit and half-chewed food!
Film: *Shrek 2*
Gross rating: 🌟🌟🌟🌟🌟

GROSS AWARD FOR SURPRISING SCRATCHING

Wearing fancy clothes made Shrek's butt itch after he and Fiona have a makeover. So he got a servant, Fiddlesworth, to itch it with a big stick!
Film: *Shrek the Third*
Gross rating: 🌟🌟🌟

GROSS AWARD FOR EXPLOSIVE BURPING

When Fergus and Felicia farted, Farkle followed it up with a big burp, which was so powerful, it exploded in the fireplace! Imagine what his burps will be like when he's grown up!
Film: *Shrek the Third*
Gross rating: 🌟🌟🌟🌟

GROSS AWARD FOR TOILET TRAUMAS

The Star Tours chariot knocks over Shrek's outhouse – while the poor guy is on the toilet!
Film: *Shrek Forever After*
Gross rating: 🌟🌟🌟🌟

29

DID YOU KNOW?

The word 'caterpillar' comes from the Latin words for 'cat' and 'hair'.

Parasites such as roundworms, hookworms, flukes and tapeworms – which can grow up to 9.75 metres long – live *inside* our bodies.

Kangaroo poo is sometimes used to make paper!

Hagfish have no eyes, jaws or stomach. One of the slimiest fish in the sea, hagfish tie themselves in a knot around dead or dying fish and bore into their flesh with a special type of tongue. How *knotty*!

Botflies are bad news for caribou (a large North American reindeer). The disgusting little bug will speed into a caribou's face (at up to 30kph!) and spray maggots at the caribou's nose. The maggots crawl up the caribou's nostrils and live in its nasal passage!

Army ants attack or eat anything that gets in their way when they're marching through a forest!

Most fleas are about 3mm long, but they can jump over 30cm, which is around 100 times their own length!

Flea

Unlike humans, a rat's teeth keep growing throughout its life. If it didn't wear them down by chewing things, its lower gnashers would end up growing through the roof of its mouth!

Rats have seriously strong teeth and can gnaw through metal, wood and electrical cables.

Hibernating together isn't always a good idea for rats – they get so cosy their tails sometimes get tangled in knots.

TRUE OR FALSE?

A rat can survive a fall from the roof of a ten-storey building.

Answer: False! Although they can fall from a five-storey building and survive, which is still pretty impressive!

Rats are really good swimmers. They can tread water for three days and swim 800 metres without stopping. Must come in handy when they're scurrying about in sewers!

Rats keep track of their temperature through their tails. If a rat is really hot, it will lie on its back to cool down. Unless Pied Piper is playing his flute, that is; then they'd have to dance to his magical music!

When it comes to clever camouflage, the *Papilio aegeus* butterfly has a gross but effective solution. The caterpillar avoids unwelcome predators by making itself look like bird droppings – white poop splattered on brown!

Camels have *three* eyelids to protect their peepers from the desert's swirling sand.

Giraffes have very long tongues – up to 56cm long – which they use to pluck food from trees and clean their noses. Slurp!

Cockroaches breathe through little holes in their sides, called spiracles.

People swallowed woodlice as a cure for tuberculosis and athletes' foot in the nineteenth century! Don't try it now!

Woodlouse

Flamingos eat algae, small insects and crustaceans, which is what turns their feathers pink.

Hippos whirl their tail round when they're pooping, so it flies everywhere and marks their territory. Messy but effective!

A deep sea gulper eel can eat a fish that is larger than itself – its jaw bends back 180 degrees!

Forget breast-feeding, the babies of the boulengerula taitanus eat their mother's flesh! The worm-like amphibian's babies have special teeth when they're born and wriggle over their mother, chomping on her skin.

Whales vomit around once a week to get rid of anything indigestible they've eaten.

←Hippo toilet

TRUE OR FALSE?
The werewolf finch is a bird that has a habit of pecking at other birds and feeding on their blood.

Answer: False! There's no such thing as a werewolf finch – there is a vampire finch that does this though!

SHREK'S CRAZY MAZE!

Guide Shrek through the maze to help Fiona with the kids.
But watch out for the crazy critters and yucky splats!

DID YOU KNOW?

Bored monkeys often throw their poop at people to keep themselves entertained.

When it's attacked, the bombadier beetle fires a cloud of nasty brown gas out of its bum in rapid squirts. The disgusting gas blinds attackers and lets the beetle escape! Nifty!

The *Hyla vasta* is the world's largest tree frog. This slimy little critter has huge round finger- and toe-discs which grip like superglue.

An octopus will eat its own tentacles if it becomes distressed.

When it's eating a big meal, the viperfish moves all its internal organs to the back of its body to make room for the food!

The duckbilled platypus can stuff its mouth with up to 600 worms at once. Bet they don't speak with their mouth full though!

If it has no food, the ribbon worm can eat up to 95 per cent of its own body to survive!

Octopus

Got sleep in your eye? Spare a thought for cows. There's a gross bug, called the face fly, that loves eating the mucus in a cow's peepers.

Moths love nothing more than tucking into a filthy woolly jumper. The dirtier it is, the better! The fluttery little fellas especially love wool covered in sweat and food!

Honeybees have a very strange way of dealing with intruders. They surround any unwanted guests in their colony and vibrate their bodies, which causes so much heat, the invader is *cooked*!

Face flies

A peckish carrion beetle will squirt digestive juices over a snail's shell, then suck out and eat the snail's body!

Vampire bats need to eat every day, or they die. If one of the critters can't find food, it makes another bat vomit and eats that instead!

TRUE OR FALSE?
Birds don't urinate.
Answer: True! Their wee and poo are mixed together – which is why bird poo is so slimy!

←*Bird* poo

DONKEY'S CRAZY
CREATURE JOKES

1 What's small, cuddly and
bright purple?
A koala holding his breath!

2 What do you call a frog with
no hind legs?
Unhoppy!

3 What did the slug say as he fell
off a branch?
"How slime flies!"

4 Why are elephants so wrinkly?
Have you ever tried to iron one?

5 What's a polygon?
A dead parrot!

6 How do you find where
a flea has bitten you?
Start from scratch!

7 What is a dog's favorite sport?
Formula 1 drooling!

8 What do you call a fly with
no wings?
A walk!

9 Why are frogs so happy?
They eat whatever
bugs them!

10 How do you know it's raining
cats and dogs?
You step in a poodle!

11 How do you keep flies out
of the kitchen?
Put a pile of manure in the
living room!

12 What's the difference between
a worm and an apple?
Have you ever tried worm pie?

13 What do you give an elephant
that's going to be sick?
Plenty of space!

14 On which day do lions eat people?
Chewsday!

15 What game do elephants play
with ants?
Squash!

16 What do you get when you
sit under a cow?
A pat on the head!

17 What day do fish hate?
Fry-day!

18 How do mice feel
after a bath?
Squeaky clean!

19 What monkey is
always exploding?
A ba-boom!

20 Where do dogs go
when they lose
their tails?
The re-tail store!

← *Dribbly giraffe*

Giraffes create loads of salvia to help them swallow the leaves they eat. Be careful if you're standing near one – they tend to drool a lot!

Jackals feed their young by throwing up food they've eaten. Once the pups have had enough, the jackal will re-eat their vomit.

Mosquitoes drool special saliva on your skin to make it numb – then they feed on your blood!

Cows have four stomachs and have to sick up the grass they eat and re-chew it before they can digest it.

Because they don't have sweat glands, vultures wee on their legs when they get too hot. This not only cools them down, it kills any germs on their legs too. Wouldn't a quick dip in a birdbath be easier?!

Unwanted visitors? Don't do what fulmars do! Disturb this seabird on its nest and it will spray a big jet of fishy oil at you from a distance of over three metres!

DID YOU KNOW?

Flies vomit on food to break it down into a soupy substance they can suck up though their straw-shaped tongue. Mmm-mmm!

AWFUL ANIMALS QUIZ!

Take our test to find out how much you know about
the world's yuckiest creatures...

1 What do parrotfish
make their protective
sleeping bag out of?
a) Mucus
b) Poo
c) Sand

2 How long can a
cockroach live
without a head?
a) One day
b) At least a week
c) A whole month

3 How do sharks protect
their eyes when they
attack prey?
a) Blink a lot
b) Keep them closed
c) Roll them
backwards

4 What is kangaroo
poo sometimes used
to make?
a) Socks
b) Sweets
c) Paper

5 How do vultures
keep predators away?
a) Peck at their necks
b) Throw up in
their eyes
c) Jump on their
backs

6 How many stomachs
do cows have?
a) One
b) Four
c) Two

7 How far does the
gulper eel's jaw bend
back?
a) 180 degrees
b) 90 degrees
c) 45 degrees

8 What part of a caribou
do botflies spray
maggots at?
a) Nose
b) Ear
c) Tail

Vile vulture

*Now turn over
to see how
you scored*

ANSWERS

1a, 2b, 3c, 4c, 5b, 6b, 7a, 8a

1 TO 3 CORRECT

YOU'RE A CRAZY CREATURE – LIKE DONKEY!

You may like gross, slimy animals, but it looks like you don't know that much about them at the moment. No problem – keep reading and you'll soon know more than Donkey.

4 TO 6 CORRECT

YOU'RE ONE BRILL BEING – LIKE PUSS!

Well done! You may not have got all the answers right, but you know your parrotfish from your parasites, and your botflies from your beetles. You're on a par with Puss, who has seen plenty of gross creatures.

OVER 7 CORRECT

YOU'RE ONE COOL CRITTER – JUST LIKE SHREK!

Uh-oh! You know so much about gross creatures, are you sure you're not really an ogre?! Only joking – you may be a brainbox when it comes to the world's most disgusting critters, but you're definitely not green!

GROSS BODILY FUNCTIONS

When it comes to bodily functions, Shrek hasn't got
a problem with whipping up an earwax candle or belching
with the best of 'em. We may not be ogres but our bods
can do some seriously gross stuff too...

Farts and belches are your body's way of getting rid of unwanted air. You swallow air throughout the day, especially when you gobble up food or talk while you're eating, and your body makes gases as it digests food. Once there's gas in your body, it has to come out sooner or later!

Drinking fizzy drinks means you swallow another type of gas – carbon dioxide. This is the gas that is used to put the bubbles in pop. So when you glug down your favourite drink, you also swallow lots of carbon dioxide, which will eventually resurface as a burp or fart!

51 WAYS TO SAY FART

1 Drop one

2 Guff

3 Rear roar

4 Pump

5 Squeeze the cheese

6 Step on a frog

7 Blow your butt bugle

8 Poofume

9 Let a big windy

10 Rip one

11 Melting the south pole

12 Activating your air brakes

13 Letting off some steam

14 Beep your horn

15 Stale wind

16 Butt burp

17 Poot

18 Spreading the love

19 Ripper

20 Botty cough

21 Trumping

22 Silent but violent

23 Fartrogen dioxide

24 Blurp

25 Toot

26 Let rip

27 Honker

28 Sneeze in your pants

29 Air biscuit

30 Bottom burp

31 Back blast

32 Bean fumes

33 Blampf

34 Drifter

35 Explosion between the cheeks

36 Belly cough

37 Squeaker

38 Stinker

39 Thunderpants

40 Botty burpage

41 Silent but deadly

42 Let one go

43 Air attack

44 Backdoor trumpet

45 Cut the cheese

46 Windy pops

47 Playing the butt bassoon

48 Butt yodelling

49 Deal one

50 Parp

51 Bum hum

TRUE OR FALSE?
Astronauts aren't allowed
to eat certain food before
a space-flight in case it
gives them gas.
Answer: True!
People heading into space are
banned from scoffing things
like beans!

A burp can contain up to 80ml of gas.

In some countries burping is a way of saying 'thank you' to the chef. Nice!

It's not just humans that burp – animals do it too. Cows produce about 50 million tonnes of methane gas every year! Ewww!

Some wood-eating insects, including termites, have also been known to get gas. You'd have to listen hard to hear it though!

Everyone burps and farts. And we do it at least 10–15 times a day!

The scientific word for letting air from you stomach escape from your mouth (i.e. burping) is eructation.

Hungry termites

Think your burps are loud? The loudest belch ever recorded was 107.1 decibels, which is louder than a car horn!

Eating Brussels sprouts, onions, cabbage or beans will give you gas. So expect trumpeting in your trousers when you have them for dinner!

Farts are super-smelly when different food in your gut gets together to form a gas called hydrogen sulphide. When this happens, your farts smell like rotten eggs!

Like chomping on crisps? Well, the crunchy little critters are full of tiny air bubbles, so don't be surprised if eating them gives you gas!

You will release around 2 litres of gas from your intestines today as burps or farts.

Farty sprouts

DID YOU KNOW?

$3/4$ of your poo is made of water. The rest of the smelly stuff is made up of fibre, dead bacteria, fats, protein and dead cells.

You lose around 40,000 dead skin cells every minute, which are eaten by tiny critters that live in your bedding and clothes.

Ever wondered why we have earwax? Well the icky-looking stuff helps keep your ears clean. The greasy wax traps dust, dirt and bugs that could damage your hearing.

Your feet produce half a pint of sweat every day. No wonder your socks pong sometimes!

Cheesy feet

Your skin is covered in millions of bacteria. Some of it is bad bacteria, but some of it keeps you healthy.

Want to see the dead skin on your body? Put some sticky tape on your arm and pull it off. You'll see dead skin cells and oil stuck to the tape!

Your fingernails grow 0.05cm a week, which is four times faster than your toenails.

Saliva (spit) is made to make your food easier to swallow. It also helps you taste food. You can only taste stuff by detecting chemicals floating around in your drool!

Spit is made by six special salivary glands – two under your tongue, two under your jaw and two under your ears.

Every day your salivary glands squirt out 1–1.5 litres of drool, which you swallow.

Your saliva has some really gross ingredients, such as mucus, the stuff that streams out of your nose when you have a cold. The mucus is what makes your spit slimy and stringy!

You will produce 37,800 litres of saliva in your lifetime. That's a serious amount of spit!

Slimy saliva

There can be up to 15,000,000,000 (15 billion) bacteria in your mouth at any one time, a lot of which you end up swallowing with your spit. Good job your saliva contains chemicals that kills most bacteria and germs, so as gross as drool can be, it actually helps keep your mouth free from infection.

DID YOU KNOW?

You spray about 300 droplets of spit a minute when you are talking.

FOUL BODILY FUNCTIONS!

Could some of the foul bodily functions in *Shrek* movies happen in real life? Find out here ...

FOUL BODILY FUNCTION:
Shrek and the ogre army have eyeballs for dinner.

HAPPEN IN REAL LIFE?
Yes! People from all over the world eat eyeballs – they are considered a delicacy in some countries.

FOUL BODILY FUNCTION:
Shrek farts while he's taking a dip and the smell kills a fish!

HAPPEN IN REAL LIFE?
This wouldn't happen if we did the same thing. Ogres eat so many gross things, including rats, toads and raw fish eyes, that their farts are much smellier than ours.

FOUL BODILY FUNCTION:
Fiona has to shave her face in the morning, just like Shrek.

HAPPEN IN REAL LIFE?
This can happen in real life. Some women have naturally hairy faces. It's best not to shave like Fiona though – there are loads of better ways for a woman to remove the hair!

FOUL BODILY FUNCTION:

Shrek pulls earwax from his ear and uses it as a candle!

HAPPEN IN REAL LIFE?

It would be kind of handy (and gross!) if we could make candles from our earwax, but it's just something disgusting that ogres do. Earwax is not made from the same chemicals as the wax used in candles so it wouldn't burn in the same way. Lucky Shrek!

FOUL BODILY FUNCTION:

Shrek burps and lights it with a match, which lights his fire.

HAPPEN IN REAL LIFE?

It would be impossible to light a burp as it's just air escaping from your stomach. It's possible to light farts though, because they have different chemicals in them, but it's best not to as you could end up getting burnt.

FOUL BODILY FUNCTION:

Shrek keeps his teeth clean by squeezing green stuff out of a caterpillar and using it as toothpaste!

HAPPEN IN REAL LIFE?

No! Brushing your teeth with a squished caterpillar won't give you a dazzling smile – it would make you ill! The Romans used crushed mouse brains as toothpaste, but it's probably best not to try that either!

Most people produce 1–2 litres of urine (wee) a day. That's 40,000 litres in a lifetime – enough to fill 500 baths. That's *wee*-lly loads, isn't it?!

When your bladder fills up with wee, its sides stretch until they're as thin as an onion skin. Have a look at an onion – that's waaay thin!

Wee →

Urine is only around 96% water. The other 4% is a mix of urea (a waste chemical made by your body), waste protein and salt.

Want to know what's in snot? Well, the air you breathe in contains particles like dust and pollen. These particles are trapped in your nose by fine hairs and mucus to stop them getting into your lungs. Once the particles are trapped, the snot dries and forms bogeys! So bogeys are dried-up, dust- and germ-filled bits of snot.

Pus is made of dead bacteria and dead blood cells.

TRUE OR FALSE?

The world record for longest ear hair is over 13cm.

Answer: True! Radhakant Bajpai of Naya Ganj, India, currently holds the record. Bet he loves combing it!

You lose 100,000 brain cells every day. Luckily you have 100 billion altogether! Phew!

If the surface area of your brain could be ironed out it would measure 2,090 sq.cm.

Your nose makes aproximately a cup of snot every day!

Zits are caused by blocked pores in your skin or by bad bacteria. White blood cells rush to help heal the spot, but this forms pus, giving us the term 'white-head'. Spot on!

DID YOU KNOW?
80% of household dust is made of dead human skin!

Juicy zit

There are 50 trillion cells in your body and 3 billion of them die every minute (4,320,000,000,000 a day). Most of them are replaced – you make 10 billion new white blood cells each day.

OGRES UNCOVERED!

Think you know all about Shrek and his family?
Here's your chance to find out ...

Shrek puts out flaming torches by wetting his fingers and pinching the flame. Don't try this at home – unless you're an ogre!

An ogre's ears make brilliant battle horns or trumpets when they hold their nose and blow!

Shrek's ears are packed with ear wax – it smells really cheesy!

Shrek's teeth are stained from all of the gross things he eats. Gargling with stagnant, muddy water probably doesn't help!

Shrek's feet are super smelly. Hi toenails are really long and so tough they have to be sanded down instead of trimmed!

Like most ogres, Shrek has a very large mouth. This comes in handy when he wants to eat a whole fish or drink a pint of beer in one go.

54

Fiona has long hairs up her nose – she has to get them plucked when she has a makeover!

Ogres have such strong stubble, they can light a match by striking it on their chin.

Ogre babies love burping and farting – just as much as grown-up ogres!

Like all ogres, Fiona is pretty strong. She can move secret stone panels in the castle walls!

Fiona is a martial arts expert – she gets all her moves from her mother!

Fergus, Farkle and Felicia are pretty good at being sick on people. And their sick is green and really disgusting!

GROSS BODY JOKES

1 What colour is a burp?
Burple!

2 What has a bottom at the top?
Your legs!

3 Did you hear the joke about
the girl who farted?
You don't want to – it stinks!

4 What did one eye say to the
other eye?
"Between you and me, something
smells a lot!"

5 What did one tonsil say
to the other tonsil?
"Get dressed, the doctor
is taking us out
tonight!"

6 What did the dentist
of the year get?
A little plaque!

7 Why did the bald man paint
rabbits on his head?
Because from a distance they
looked like hares!

8 What do you call someone who
wipes his nose on his jacket?
Green sleeves!

9 What's the difference between
a Brussels sprout and a bogey?
Kids won't eat Brussels sprouts!

10 What time should you
go to the dentist?
2:30 (Tooth-hurty)!

11 Why did the boy bring toilet
paper to the party?
He was a party pooper!

12 How do you get a handkerchief
to dance?
Put a little boogie in it!

13 Why is your nose in the
middle of your face?
Because it's in the scent-er!

14 Why are false teeth like stars?
Because they come out at night!

15 Why is the human body
like a jail?
It's made of cells!

16 How do you cure a headache?
Stand in front of a window and
shut your eyes – the pane will
disappear!

17 What can you catch but
not throw?
Your breath!

18 What do you get if you eat
baked beans and onions?
Tear gas!

19 Why was the nose tired?
Because it kept running!

20 What's the perfect cure
for dandruff?
Baldness!

Think your nails get long sometimes? Shridhar Chillal of Pune, India, has been growing the nails on his left hand since 1952 – they are more than a whopping 600cm long!

TRUE OR FALSE?

The longest attack of hiccups lasted for 68 years.

Answer: True! Charles Osborne of Anthon, Iowa, USA, started hiccuping in 1922 and didn't stop until February 1990!

You lose about 0.5 litres of water a day through 3,000,000 sweat glands.

Got a cold? Well, make sure you catch your sneezes in a tissue. If you don't, you'll be spraying up to 40,000 infectious droplets into the air!

Your sneezes can travel a distance of 2 to 3 metres at speeds of up to 160kph – as fast as a train!

As many as 100 trillion viruses and bacteria live on each of us. However much we wash, there are always 10 million or so bacteria on every square centimetre of our skin.

GROSS BODILY FUNCTION QUIZ!

How much you know about your yucky body?

1 Why do we have earwax?
a) It makes our ears smell nice
b) To help keep our ears clean
c) To make our ears bendy

2 How many viruses live on most of us?
a) 100 million
b) 100 billion
c) 100 trillion

3 What is the scientific word for burping?
a) Honking
b) Burplation
c) Eructation

4 How much snot does your nose make every day?
a) A cupful
b) None
c) A whole bucket!

5 How far can your sneezes travel?
a) 1 to 2 metres
b) 2 to 3 metres
c) 3 to 5 metres

6 How many salivary glands make spit?
a) Two
b) Six
c) Four

7 What is the biggest ingredient of household dust?
a) Pollen
b) Human skin
c) Food

8 How many bacteria live on each cm² of your skin?
a) 10 million
b) 100 million
c) 1,000 million

Now turn over to see how you scored

59

GROSS BODILY FUNCTIONS

ANSWERS
1b, 2c, 3c, 4a, 5b, 6b, 7b, 8a

1 TO 3 CORRECT
YOU SMELLED IT!

You may produce as many bogeys and burps as Shrek does, but you don't seem to know that much about bodily functions yet. Don't worry – keep reading, and you'll soon love farts and fungus as much as the famous green ogre!

4 TO 6 CORRECT
YOU FELT IT!

Good work! You may not know everything about gross bodily functions, but you still know quite a bit! You almost know as much about oozing, dripping and whiffing as Shrek – you'll soon be bathing in swamp mud at this rate!

OVER 7 CORRECT
YOU DEALT IT!

Yay! When it comes to gross bodily functions, you really know what's what. Shrek and Fiona have got nothing on you – you're a burping, farting and smelly earwax genius!